IN THE MOMENT

365 CREATIVE WAYS
TO CONNECT
WITH YOUR WORLD

JOCELYN DE KWANT

ILLUSTRATED BY
SANNY VAN LOON

ABRAMS NOTERIE, NEW YORK

Text © 2018 Jocelyn de Kwant
Illustrations © 2018 Sanny van Loon/Shop Around
Design and layout © 2018 Quarto Publishing plc
Cover design © 2018 Abrams

ISBN: 978-1-4197-3077-1

This book was conceived, designed, and produced by
Leaping Hare Press
An imprint of The Quarto Group
The Old Brewery, 6 Blundell Street
London N7 9BH, United Kingdom
T (0)20 7700 6700 F (0)20 7700 8066
www.quartoknows.com

Printed and bound in China

10 9 8 7 6 5 4 3 2 1

Abrams Noterie products are available at special discounts
when purchased in quantity for premiums and promotions
as well as fundraising or educational use. Special editions
can also be created to specification. For details, contact
specialsales@abramsbooks.com or the address below.

ABRAMS The Art of Books
195 Broadway, New York, NY 10007
abramsbooks.com

Contents

Introduction

As a kid, were you always embracing the now, drawing for hours, completely forgetting the world around you, lying on your bed looking at the shadows your hands made in the light, or discovering insects in the backyard? It felt very normal to be nowhere else but in that moment, unaware of how special that was, something to cherish. But as we get older, those moments happen less and less often. By the time we're in our twenties, we're always running from one place to another. We simply don't have time to be in the moment: When we're at work we're thinking of home and when we're at home we're thinking of work. We are always worrying about what we have to do, or if we should have said or done something differently. It's so, so stressful to live this way.

When I was twenty-five, I was diagnosed with burnout. Back then I knew no one who was burned out. What was happening? I couldn't do anything any more. I had panic attacks at night and my stomach was hurting all the time. I was tired, so tired I couldn't even read a book. I was ordered by my doctor to stay home and recover and it took me months to get back on my feet. I went to a therapist a lot and I slept a lot. But I also started to go on long hikes; every day at the same time, I'd walk for three hours. And I took up crafting again, something I loved as a kid, but had completely stopped doing. Little by little I felt better. When I was finally functioning once more, I made myself a promise: never to let it happen again.

I read all there was to read about stress and burnouts. But I also tried to keep doing what had calmed me down during my weeks at home: going out in nature and doing something just for me every day. The good thing was that, as an editor for women's magazines, I got to try out lots of different things and speak to interesting people. I collected wisdom and scientific research like baseball cards for a collector's album. When I started to work for *Flow Magazine* in 2008, I was in my element:

a magazine about creativity and positive psychology. One of their key topics is mindfulness, and discovering mindfulness for me was life-changing. It made so much sense to me. If I had discovered mindfulness when I was younger, I might never have burned out. If I had been more mindful back then, I would have noticed that I wasn't doing so well long before I could do nothing at all. I would have had more moments of relaxation and inner peace. I would have been more at ease with my situation, instead of trying to fix things or always looking forward.

But there was something else I discovered on my journey. There are so many people out there like me: people who are tired of the rat race; people who want to slow down and be creative again, who want to create things with their hands instead of a computer; men and women who find that there is more to life than making money and running from A to B; people who—like me—struggle to embrace the moment. But as with many things, writing about it and researching it didn't make it easier to practice it.

So, here's what I did. I decided to take a couple of minutes every day and do one thing with my complete attention. I know mindfulness is so much more than that, but it was at least something I could schedule. Soon I found out that it was easiest for me to stay in the moment when I was creating something: drawing or writing or crafting. And the more often I scheduled in moments like that, the more it became second nature. Those little moments during the day help to ground and calm us down in stressful periods. Because that's the way life is, I guess; there will always be stressful moments.

I wrote down everything that helped me in this little book: to create a moment of awareness every day, to draw, create, connect, and flourish. Some prompts are simple, some are just for fun, some are insights from wise people that've helped me, but they're all about focusing on little things and appreciating the present moment to help your creativity flow. Sometimes you just need to feel like you're seven years old again and don't have any cares. Sometimes you need to lie on your back and look at the shadows.

NATURE

I GO TO NATURE TO BE SOOTHED AND HEALED,

AND TO HAVE MY SENSES PUT IN ORDER

I couldn't agree more with these words of American essayist **John Burroughs** (1837–1921). Nature is hands down the best place to calm the mind. Sunlight shattering over the water; birds singing; the sound of leaves in the wind; even just writing it down gives me a good feeling.

We don't need scientific research to tell us that spending time in nature is good for us; we can feel it in every bone of our bodies. Nevertheless, research has shown that spending time in nature makes us less impulsive, relaxes us, makes us more helpful and more creative. We feel less physical pain when surrounded by nature, less alone and isolated, and kids thrive from being in nature, the list goes on and on.

We're not meant to spend every day between bricks and asphalt, so obviously scientists from all over the world urge city people to spend more time in nature. Spending too little time in our beautiful natural surroundings causes problems to our health and mental well-being.

The Japanese custom of *Forest Bathing*, where people spend deliberate time in forests, was found to reduce stress and improve health. The good news is that you don't have to go hiking in the woods to improve your well-being. If you are mindful of the natural objects and elements that surround you on a daily basis, you are already benefiting from nature's power. Birds flying in the sky; water life in small ponds and canals; clouds drifting by; the moon; it can even be as simple as appreciating that little flower that grows through a crack in the concrete. Just look around you and open your eyes to the beauty of it all.

1 Just as we close our eyes when night falls, most flowers close their petals until dawn signals the birth of another day. Go out at dusk and look for a common flower when opened and closed.

Draw it here.

2 Bugs are great. Take pill bugs, for example: if you touch them they roll up into a little ball. They are working hard to change old leaves into healthy soil. Find a ground bug and study it for a while.

Make notes here.

3 Have you ever noticed that each blueberry has a little flower shape on top?

Look for another unexpected flower around you and draw it here.

4 Find a tree leaf and draw it on this page. Note five things about it, such as its shape, color, and texture.

5 Every spider is an artist, spinning its silky
architecture in the corners of our lives.

Finish this spider's web between these two branches.

6

Find a little feather.
Glue it on this page. Note the date
and the place you found it.

Date: ....

Place: ....

GLUE
HERE

7 Describe a moment when you felt completely at one with nature.

How old were you? Where were you? How did you feel?

8 Go out into nature and collect a range of different fallen flower petals and leaves of all sizes, shapes, and colors.

Use them to create your own imaginary flower and stick it to this page.

9 Watching a sunset with our full attention evokes emotion and calms us down, whether we're alone or with a loved one. It's just the way we're wired. Watching a sunset even slows down our perception of time. Good thing the sun sets every day. Allow your mind to drift back to a sunset that was special to you.

Where were you? How did it make you feel?

....
....
....
....
....
....
....
....
....
....
....
....

10 Even in our towns and cities, where bricks and concrete dominate, the wilderness can find us. Go out in search of wild flowers growing between the cracks of the pavement.

Where did you find one?

11 Go spider-hunting in your home, garden, or beyond and find one to draw. Pay special attention to its uniqueness: What pattern is on its back? How do its legs move?

Notice and record the fine details.

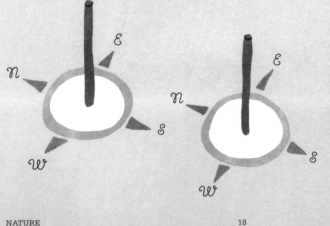

12 Sundials may have been relegated to the history books, but there is much to learn in the shadows.

Place a stick in the ground in the sunshine and note how the shadow changes throughout the day—draw it at two different times on these sundials.

13 Sketch a piece of fruit with as much accuracy as possible. What new things do you notice?

14 Rainforest frogs often have bright, vibrant colors and beautiful markings to indicate (or pretend) that they are poisonous. In the Amazon, more than 1,000 species can be found.

Make up some wild coloring and patterns for these frogs.

15 Find a peaceful place to quiet your mind and listen to the sounds of nature talking to you.

Jot down what you can hear if you ignore all human sounds.

16 It's difficult not to smile when faced with a peacock and its elaborate fan of colorful, theatrical feathers.

Draw some fancy tail feathers for this peacock.

17 Leaves come in so many shapes. Find as many different ones as you can and draw around them here. Make patterns using their different outlines.

Try to find out what kind of tree, bush, or flower they came from.

18 The calming effect of nature is so strong that even looking at a painting of nature can be relaxing.

Finish this tree and color it in. While working on it, focus only on coloring. If your mind starts to wander, bring your attention back to the page.

19 Cut some tree leaves in different shapes and glue them on the page.

20
Find a flower you like.
When the flower dies, collect the seeds
and make sure they're dry.

*Put the seeds in a little paper bag,
fold over the top, and draw the flower on
the outside; they're ready for you to sow
next year in a garden or pot.*

21 Collect two different flowers and dry them. Place them between two paper towels, put them inside an old book, and stack a couple of heavy books on top. After two weeks, take out your pressed flowers and glue them to this page.

Date found

....

Where

....

Notes

....

....

....

....

....

....

....

....

....

Date found

....

Where

....

Notes

....

....

....

....

....

....

....

....

....

....

22 If you know more, you will see more. Investigate an ordinary wild flower. What is its Latin name? What are its special characteristics?

Note your findings here.

NOTES

23 Lie back and look up at the sky. What do you notice?

Take notes here and then repeat after two hours to see what's changed.

24 Staring into the flames of a fire can make your thoughts more philosophical, according to the French philosopher Gaston Bachelard (1884–1962). While watching the dancing flames, your mind may start to wander and reach new depths.

Draw flames on these wooden logs and allow your mind to drift.

25

Bring some outside nature inside. Pluck some long grass or simple common flowers and put them in a little jar or vase.

26 Little bugs: Where do they come from? Where do they go?

Go outside to find an insect and fantasize about its life story as you watch its activities.

27 Nature can move us deeply—its endless cycles of birth and decay, its beauty and ferocity, its simplicity and complexity.

Think of something that fascinates you about nature. What is the first thing that comes to mind?

28 Give a big tree a closer look. Notice the different kinds of moss growing on it. Is it only growing on the shadowy side? How many different shades of green and other colors does the moss have?

Note or draw your findings.

29 Leaf through a random nature book and write down the first two sentences that spark something inside of you.

30 Go outside. Take a moment to allow yourself to truly experience the nature around you.

Notice how it makes you feel.

31 Sea snails are magical creatures. They attract calcium from the water to build their houses as protection. The ones without houses have bright colors to scare predators.

Make these snails more fantastical by giving them fancy houses and vibrant colors.

32 Look for flowers that are blossoming now in your backyard or a park. See if you can find the same type of flower at different stages: bud, bloom, and wilted.

Organize them in the right order and use tape or glue to paste them on this page.

DAILY LIFE

ENJOY THE EVERYDAY

I used to focus only on holidays, weekend trips, and special events. The Mondays and Wednesdays went by without note; they were the "in between days," wasting time until the next fun event, not important enough to really pay attention to. But one day it hit me that those ordinary days form the greatest part of our lives. We spend far more time doing our usual daily stuff than going on adventures.

The moment I started to pay attention to the ordinary days, I started to appreciate them much more – the magic of little things: clean sheets on the bed, the way the sunbeams enter the living room, a bath. Paying more attention to the details makes simple days more meaningful.

Daily life is very underappreciated; we don't necessarily have to go sightseeing in a different country to discover new things; when we look at our own neighborhoods with the eyes of a tourist it's just as exciting.

It's easy to forget and slip into our old unaware ways, but there are always means of helping us to stay mindful of the small moments that life is made up of:

- *Put your phone away when you don't really need it.*
- *Put your phone away when you think you need it (but actually don't).*
- *Try to keep a "beginner's mind" and don't take things for granted.*
- *Do one thing at a time (and stop the endless multitasking).*
- *Move away from the idea that the next moment is more important than this one.*
- *Start to see the daily things as a source of inspiration.*

Being mindful and appreciative of daily life puts a little sparkle on everything. And it costs far less than a weekend trip.

33 Pick three simple tools that you use regularly—in your work, in your kitchen, or study—and draw them. Create a decorative pattern by playing with the images and drawing them in a different order.

Tiny Pleasures

34 Forget about skydiving; make a bucket list of tiny daily pleasures. Keep your wishes as small—and achievable—as possible. What would you like to do or experience more of?

35
Draw your groceries from today.

36 What is your favorite day of the week and why?

Mon   Thu
Tue   Fri
Wed   Sat Sun

37 Where would we be without our favorite jeans or sweater? Give the items of clothing you love a place on the podium.

Draw one each in first, second, and third place.

38 There is always something to appreciate about your ordinary day, even if your routine seems monotonous and you live for the weekend—you just have to look for it!

Make two quick sketches of what you like about a typical day.

39 Draw your daily route to work, school, or your other daily obligations (*or all of the above*). Pay extra attention to the parts that you enjoy about your daily route.

40 Liven up your daily chores by putting on some music. It's a small change that can make a big difference. You might even end up dancing on a Monday morning.

Jot down four of your favorite energizing songs.

41 STOP!
Breathe.

Write down how you are feeling right now.

42 Draw your favorite person from your neighborhood.

EMPLOYEE OF THE MONTH

43 Close your eyes. When you open them, engage your "beginner's mind"; look around you as if you are seeing everything for the first time.

What are the first things that you notice?

44 A compliment doesn't have to come from your boss, partner, or friends to put a smile on your face and keep the positivity circulating.

Write yourself a compliment.

YOU DESERVE IT.

45

Wisdom is everywhere.
Read a random magazine or newspaper article,
blog post or website, with your complete attention.
Find some wisdom in it, a sentence that
fits your life right now.

Write it down here.

....
....
....
....
....
....
....
....

46 Describe your weekday morning routine in words and/or pictures.

Think of three ways to shake up the routine.

47 A "no" to trivial distractions is a "yes" to a more focused and fulfilling day. Name some of the trivial distractions that occur during your usual day.

Me.

48 There are probably many people you don't really know who form part of your daily routine and you form part of theirs. With yourself in the middle of this space, draw interlocking circles, like a Venn diagram, to champion the people with whom you share your existence: work colleagues, your kids' friends, your yoga teacher, people you see at the train station.

49 Shake up your everyday space. Draw a plan of your living room, then have fun thinking about how you could rearrange it. Maybe with a cozy corner for your favorite reading chair.

50 Focus only on positive things today. Jot down or draw five positive things right now. Notice how focusing on the positive affects your mood.

1   2   3   4   5

51 What songs would you include in a "Day in My Life" soundtrack? Write your favorite lyrics here.

52 Imagine the front wall has disappeared from an apartment complex or house that you know.

Draw the little household scenes that are happening behind it.

53 People feel most at home when their surroundings reflect their life stories and say something about who they are —pictures of special moments, souvenirs, subtle reminders of beloved grandparents, things like that. What objects in your house tell something about your life story?

Describe or draw them.

54 The media tends to focus on negative news. Check today's newspaper and look for something positive that happened.

Cut and paste the headline here.

55 Pick a daily task and do it in slow motion. Notice what happens with your thoughts as well as your execution of the task.

56

There is something calming about watching fresh laundry fluttering in the wind.

Fill this washing line with a soothing array of clothing.

57 Take a close look at something you're wearing. There's a strong possibility that it's either knitted or woven. In the old days, this fine art was greatly appreciated.

Look closely at the structure of the fabric and try drawing it.

58 Make up a little poem about your day.

59 Imagine you are an alien visiting from outer space and your home is the subject of an investigation.

Report to your planet about the daily lives of the inhabitants.

60 Draw your daily means of transport—car, subway, train—but instead of using its real colors, have fun by giving it bright, happy colors.

61 Noticing everything you have to be thankful for can boost your well-being and even improve your health and sleep. But it can be difficult to stay in that mindset and remember the importance of gratitude. It helps if you give it a place in your evening routine.

Try noting three things you are grateful for every day for the next week.

DAY 1: Today I am grateful for

DAY 2: Today I am grateful for

DAY 3: Today I am grateful for

DAY 4: Today I am grateful for

DAY 5: Today I am grateful for

DAY 6: Today I am grateful for

DAY 7: Today I am grateful for

PLAY

YOU'RE NEVER TOO OLD FOR PLAY!

Remember how you could play for hours as a child: inventing new worlds with whatever toys were around, making little books out of paper, playing hide-and-seek at sunset with kids in the neighborhood? Even a simple bike ride could turn into something more interesting when made into a game.

Sadly, most of us stop playing as we grow older. We feel embarrassed, we're just too tired and even if those things aren't holding us back, there's always something more important to do. Isn't there? The thing is, play is still very important even when you've reached adulthood.

Stuart Brown—a pioneer in play research—says: "Nothing lights up the brain like play. Three-dimensional play fires up the cerebellum, puts a lot of impulses into the frontal lobe—the executive portion—[and] helps contextual memory be developed."

Wonderful things happen in your brain when you're playing. The act of play stimulates your creativity and problem-solving skills, and you just feel better. Or, as Brown puts it,

"The opposite of play is not work, it's depression."

So, what should we do? Learn how to play bridge, or dust off our dolls? You can, but it's not necessary. The definition of play is doing something just because you like doing it, without having a goal in mind. It's doing something unexpected that makes you laugh; it's creating something without wanting it to be the best; it's playing a game, dancing, and laughing for no reason.

The weird thing for us grownups is that we're so focused on being efficient, we hardly take the time to have fun. The following chapter is packed with simple ways to return some playfulness to your daily life. Your brain wants you to.

62 What were your favorite things to do when you were a kid?

Note them down here and pick one to do right now.

63 Play can be as simple as finding the unusual in things that are familiar and finding joy in the mundane—words, for example, are an endless source of play.

Invent a new word by putting two words together.

64 It can be so refreshing to do something that has no use whatsoever. Cut out some famous faces from a magazine and glue them here.

Have fun by drawing beards, mustaches, hats, and glasses on them.

65 Draw a maze on this page. Start with yourself and end at the hammock to represent your journey towards mindfulness and relaxation. Make it complicated.

Maybe draw some real-life stresses in there, too.

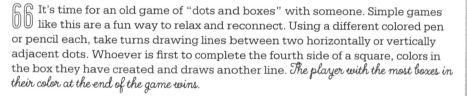

66 It's time for an old game of "dots and boxes" with someone. Simple games like this are a fun way to relax and reconnect. Using a different colored pen or pencil each, take turns drawing lines between two horizontally or vertically adjacent dots. Whoever is first to complete the fourth side of a square, colors in the box they have created and draws another line. *The player with the most boxes in their color at the end of the game wins.*

67 Imagining that things have human personalities can be a fun way of looking at the world around you. Draw one of your plants and create a personality for it. Give it a name and write a description of its character traits!

Name:
One-Eyed Joe
Personality:
Fierce & thirsty

68 What can you still remember from playing your first computer games?

Draw characters from the games of your childhood.

69 Playing keeps you young at heart. Next time you pass a playground, try one of the swings and swing like a seven-year-old. How high can you go?

Draw yourself on this swing.

70 A flight attendant who couldn't stand doing the boring safety routine the same way every flight decided to make a rap out of it. Brighten up your day by making a rap or song out of something you need to say daily.

71 The human mind is a connection machine. Challenge your creativity with a little game of associations. Start with the word "play" and write the first word you associate with it. After that, write a word you associate with the second word, and so on. *Write as many words as you can in two minutes.*

PLAY

72 Make a playful garland by cutting a string of connecting paper dolls out of a sheet of folded paper. *Give them colorful outfits and maybe some faces, too.*

73 Ever seen the face of Elvis in a slice of toast? No? Someone somewhere has because there are faces all around us —in wall sockets, the lights of the car, in food. They can be funny or creepy or weird faces. If you look around you'll find them and then you'll start noticing them everywhere.

Take pictures or draw them here.

74 Doing something with your left hand when you normally use your right hand (or the other way around) wakes up your brain.

Write a paragraph about your day with your "other" hand.

75 Get dirty!
Paint with your fingers.

76 Our best teachers in play are small children: the way they can see worlds where we see nothing; the way they can get excited about the things we take for granted. Get involved in kids' play today. Try to see what they see and learn from it.

Jot down notes about your findings.

....
....
....
....
....
....
....
....

77 Sports are about more than staying fit; if you're not having fun while exercising, you've chosen the wrong kind of sport. Maybe playing badminton on the street with a neighbor is more your thing, or dancing in your living room, or biking in nature. Write down three activities that you think you'd enjoy or have already brought you joy in the past.

Pick one to do this week.

1 ....
2 ....
3 ....

78 There's nothing more exciting than the idea of a hideout way up in the trees for just you and your friends, with a secret password and a wealth of stories that spark the imagination. Design your own treehouse to play, retreat, and imagine in. Think of any extras, like a slide or a basket to pull up treasure and midnight snacks.

79 Invent a new ride for a theme park and draw it here. What is the theme of the ride? How many loops does it have? What could be an extra selling point?

80 Add excitement to a boring day. Pretend you're working as a spy. Check the newspaper and billboards for hidden messages, creep around and imagine people you meet could be allies or rivals.

81 Watch an episode of a soap opera on television with the sound turned off, preferably with a friend. Have fun imagining what's being said and dubbing the words with strange voices.

82
What does fun mean to you? Really think about it. What activities make you light-hearted and playful?
What makes you laugh?

Add color to this snow globe with Hansel and Gretel's candy house inside.

83

84 Make a wild, eccentrically decorated cake. Put all your favorite sweet ingredients on it. Make it as crazy as you can. Invite your friends and neighbors to help you eat it.

Sketch your plans for the cake here.

85

Today, I celebrate ....

Happy Trees Day!
Merry Friendshipmas!
Celebrate something today.
Make your own confetti with colored
paper and glue some to this page.

Finish the sentence in the banner.

86 Making and listening to music score high as activities that make people happy. Did you know that rhythm is a fundamental human feature? We automatically recognize certain rhythmic patterns in music and can clap along. Not only does music give us a good feeling, but it also shows that we share a connection.

Put on some music and clap along.

87 Invent a new dance. Try different moves, which could be inspired by anything: a daily thing you do, even an animal (Do the crab! Do the bird!). When it makes you laugh and gives you a good feeling, you've got it.

Draw the moves and give your dance a name.

88 Remember as kids how we used to love collecting things, like baseball cards, or stickers, or little stones? Collect something small, like lost buttons you find or paperclips.

Draw your mini collection here.

89 You can play with just about anything at any time —even while reading the newspaper, when maybe you're thinking you should be serious.

Black out words with a marker to make funny sentences or a little poem with the remaining words. Write the best ones here.

....
....
....
....
....
....
....
....
....
....
....

90 Did you ever play hopscotch as a kid? Why did you stop? Go outside and draw a game of hopscotch on the sidewalk with chalk.

Play it yourself or invite people or kids to play with you.

91 Have fun with sidewalk chalk. Make a colorful drawing and maybe write a poem or friendly message in front of your house for the people passing by.

92 Draw as if you are a five-year-old.

BODY

ONE OF OUR BIGGEST MISCONCEPTIONS

IS THAT MIND AND BODY FUNCTION SEPARATELY

No matter how much research shows that what we think and how we feel is influenced by hormones and other body processes, lots of people still think that the whole mind-body connection belongs in the spiritual, alternative corner. Taking care of your body is even frowned upon by many intellectuals. A Buddhist teacher once told me, "You look at the world only with your head and you forget about the rest. It is such a waste of that magnificent human body."

It's all connected. Hormones shape our thoughts and emotions. Our brains register what's happening in our posture, breathing, muscles, and so on. And the other way around—information is going back and forth. Being unaware of the mind-body connection is also a missed opportunity. In the past, when I felt bad, it didn't even occur to me that it could have had something to do with the fact that I didn't take care of myself, didn't exercise or eat well, or that I was ignoring my stress and fatigue. But now it does and it has changed my life.

Your body is there to tell you how you're doing, not only physically but also emotionally. As mental coach Aaldrik Jager, a former lieutenant in the army, explains, "All emotions begin in your body. Angst, anger, happiness, sadness; the basic emotions are felt first before you can argue. But if you're only in your head, you're not feeling the signals of your body, or you disregard them. If you pay attention to them and take the signals seriously, you can take better care of yourself."

So, dance, move, breathe, and be aware of the signals your body sends. Connecting with your body is essential for feeling good and maintaining creative flow.

93 Think back to a moment this week when you were bursting with energy. *Describe the circumstances.*

What were you doing?

What time was it?

What else?

94 Try to think of a moment when you felt completely drained of energy. *Describe the circumstances.*

What happened before you felt that way?

What time was it?

What else?

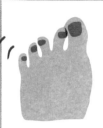
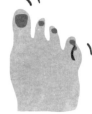

95 Wiggle your toes! Note your thoughts and feelings.

96 Have you ever watched the wonder of a baby discovering their hands for the first time? It's a magical moment and one that's too easily forgotten. Stop what you're doing right now and pay attention to your hands for a minute. Notice the shapes of the fingers, the way they move, the lines and veins that make you unique. Fill in this outline with your findings.

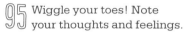

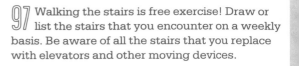

97 Walking the stairs is free exercise! Draw or list the stairs that you encounter on a weekly basis. Be aware of all the stairs that you replace with elevators and other moving devices.

98 Strike a victory pose or a superhero pose for two minutes. Research has shown that people actually feel more confident after striking confident poses. According to Amy Cuddy, of Harvard Business School, it increases testosterone levels and lowers cortisol (stress hormone) levels.

Note your own findings.

....
....
....
....
....
....
....
....
....
....
....
....

99 Wiggle your fingers! *Note your thoughts and feelings.*

100

Pull up your shoulders and drop them again. Repeat three times. Notice the difference before and after.

101

A great way to create body awareness is with dance isolations. Put on some upbeat music and sit down on a bench. First only tap your feet to the beat. After that, just move your shoulders. Then do the same with your hips, head, and so on. Try to stay in the moment, let go of all thoughts, and notice what happens in your body.

102 At night, our brain resets, or as one scientific study put it: At night, our brain is washed clean. Research has shown that a good night's sleep is just as important for you as healthy food and exercise. You don't feel well if you don't sleep enough. How do you react to a bad night's sleep?

Draw little emojis to illustrate.

103 Draw your bed. Is there anything you would change to help you sleep better?

4-7-8-Whoosh!

104
Andrew Weil is an American doctor who invented the 4-7-8 exercise, which helps to encourage sleep. It's simple. Breathe in silently for four seconds, hold your breath for seven seconds, and breathe out through your mouth for eight seconds, making a "whoosh" sound. Repeat four to eight times.

It will help you relax quickly.

105 Rediscover your biological clock. Organize an evening without screens and social events and dim the light. Notice when you start to feel tired or cold, a sign that your body is preparing for sleep. Go to bed as soon as you feel sleepy, without checking your phone or putting on an alarm clock. What time did you go to bed? At what time do you wake up? How many hours did you sleep? Try this a couple of times to see how many hours you sleep when nature takes its course.

Try to sleep that number of hours every night.

106 The blue light that our phones and computers emit keeps us awake and prevents our brains from producing the hormones that we need to fall asleep. Switch off all screens an hour before you go to sleep. Do something offline instead.

Think of three things to do:

1 ....
....
....
....
....

2 ....
....
....
....
....

3 ....
....
....
....
....

107 You might check your appearance in the mirror all the time, but how often do you really look, paying attention to the unique details that make up your face? Look in the mirror and draw one of your eyes as accurately as possible, including little black spots and small red veins.

108 Stop! What parts of your body are holding tension right now? Take a deep breath and let the tension go.

Note your findings.

109

Write a letter to your body. When did it help you? When did it hold you back? What are you grateful for? What would you say to it if it could understand you?

Be kind and pretend that you're talking to a good friend.

110 When you laugh, your brain produces endorphins, your muscles relax, and stress hormones are reduced. That's why you feel so relieved after a good laugh. Dr. Madan Kataria, the originator of laughter yoga, discovered that the human mind can't tell the difference between a real laugh and a fake laugh, so get laughing! Set the alarm for two minutes and fill the time laughing.

Note what happens.

111 Investigate your own laugh. Draw it using colors and movements that represent the sounds and special traits of *your unique, personal laugh.*

112 Smile and breathe in your happiness for a couple of minutes.

Draw a smile.

113 Try out different laughs and note how each makes you feel.

Laugh 1: Laugh as if you were a king or queen, and wave to the people.

Laugh 2: Laugh as if you were a witch; look mean and release high-pitched laughter.

Laugh 3: Laugh like a giant while taking big, heavy steps; place your hands on your stomach and feel the deep roar.

114 Buddhists believe in the divine triangle, with energy, breath, and thought in the three corners. They are separate but connected, and together they affect your whole being. It's sometimes difficult to control your thoughts and energy is also hard to control, but you **can** control your breathing.

Try to notice how different your breathing is when you're stressed from when you're relaxed.

115 For energy, try breathing in for eight seconds and out for four seconds. Repeat for one minute. Your body will be energized. To calm down, do it the other way around.

Try both breathing techniques and note the difference.

116 This yoga exercise will also fill you with energy. Breathe in and out through your nose as quickly as you can.

Keep doing this for one minute and note the outcome.

117 Breathe in, breathe out. Pause. During the pause, draw something small. Only start breathing again when your body asks you to. Repeat breathing in, breathing out, and drawing something in the break between two breaths.

118 All our emotions resonate in the body, but most of the time we are too disconnected to notice. Think of something that upsets you. Try to notice where in your body you feel that emotion.

119 When we consider the wonder of the human body, we begin to realize how miraculous we really are. How the body repairs itself when wounded is just one small miracle. Look at the human body as if you were a visitor from outer space.

What else would you find interesting about it?

120 Lie down for a meditative body scan. With every breath, concentrate on a different part of your body, starting at your toes, ending with the top of your head. Try to relax every muscle along the way. Draw arrows on the body on this page to note the areas where you found it hard to let tension go.

121 Perform a second body scan at a different time and again note where you found it hard to let tension go.

Did you notice a difference?

DOODLE

LET YOUR CREATIVITY FLOW WITH SOME RANDOM DRAWING

AND DOODLING

There are a million reasons why
I like drawing and doodling. Not because
I'm good at it. Not at all, in fact. But a long
time ago I decided to let go of the idea that
my drawings needed to look good. That
helped a lot. Nobody is paying me to draw,
so how and what I draw is totally up to
me. I'm free. And even so, I know a lot of
illustrators who became really successful
with their own weird style. In these digital
times, people crave authenticity, so
whenever my drawings are a bit off,
I just say to myself,
"Hey, at least they're authentic."

Almost every day I make a sketch about
my day in my notebook. When I don't know
what to draw, I just draw whatever is in
front of me. What do I like about this?

First, that it calms me like nothing else does. I can disappear in my own mind and forget my worries. Sometimes I notice that I'm giggling and making weird faces, matching the drawings I'm working on. I like it when something unexpected happens, when my hand does things that my mind didn't consciously tell it to. Second, I love how a doodle can be anything. Your only limitation is your own fantasy. Third, drawing and painting make me more mindful.

"You haven't really seen something unless you've drawn it,"

said the legendary Dutch illustrator **Peter Vos** (1935–2010). His favorite objects to draw were birds. "They are incredibly beautiful. And because I've drawn them, I know just how beautiful."
This chapter is full of prompts to loosen you up and challenge you to let go of expectations. Stay away from erasers or correction fluid. Laugh about your mistakes and don't hold yourself back. Let your hand scribble loosely across the page, play with it, and have fun.

122 Draw your day without letting your hand leave the page. As soon as the tip of your pencil leaves the page, you're done.

123 Draw a simple self-portrait with your right hand if you're left-handed, or the other way around if you're right-handed.

ME

124 Make these socks a little bit less boring. *Create designs for them.*

125 Fill these pots with cacti, adding flowers to some.

126 Fill this space with colorful dots.

Use magic markers, if you like.

127 Draw as many facial expressions as you can in one minute, one in each of these frames. For example: scared, in love, angry, happy, sad. Set the alarm on your phone.

Ready, set, go!

128 We all have an inner critic telling us that what we make isn't good enough. Give your inner critic a face by drawing it here. Then lock it up by drawing bars over it and throwing away the key.

129 Look beyond the normal tendency to create attractive art and make an ugly drawing. Challenge yourself to let go of all aesthetics. *Have fun with it.*

130 Practice loosening up your hand by turning on some funky music and doodling random shapes and lines while your hand moves to the music.

131

If you have ever been near a coral reef, you will know how diverse and colorful underwater life can be.

Draw different kinds of fish and sea animals here, using bright colors.

DOODLE

132 Can you draw a straight line without the aid of a ruler? *Draw ten straight lines*. It helps if you focus on where you want the line to end.

133 Stimulate your imagination by simply combining two things in one drawing that could never go together in the real world, like a bear with a cup of tea or a fish with a mustache.

Experiment with the strangest combinations.

134 Draw three different stages of an apple: whole, partially eaten, and the core.

135

Doodle some little objects in 3D.
Try starting with something simple like a small
box, then experiment with different shapes,
like a pencil or a coin.

136 The Dutch illustrator and graphic designer Dick Bruna (1927–2017), the creator of the character Miffy, was a master in simplifying the world around him. He tried to use the fewest number of lines possible, making sure the result was still recognizable. Replicating Bruna's style, draw something in front of you, then draw it again, leaving some details out. Simplify it until you can't take anything else out.

137 Draw a building in your street. Focus on the outer lines—the lines that separate the building from the sky. This will help you think about the space the building occupies, rather than just what it looks like.

138 Sometimes the simplest ideas are the most effective and fun. Try out this concept by constructing animals from basic shapes, like circles, squares, rectangles, and triangles.

139 Mindful doodling. Fill this space with spirals; don't leave any white spaces. Try to focus only on your hand on the paper. If your mind starts to wander, bring it back to the page. *Spiral away!*

DOODLE

140 As illustrator Peter Vos said, "You haven't really seen something unless you've drawn it." Draw some birds from different angles, such as, from underneath, from above, and so on.

141 Close your eyes and draw the first thing that comes to mind.

142 Create a landscape by only doodling lines, stripes, dots, crosses, and dashes with a fine-point pen. When you're done, add some trees and small houses.

143 Draw a friendly animal you know.

144 Draw a scary animal you know.

145 Draw something near you in black and white using as many lines as possible.

146 Make your day into a tiny cartoon.

147 Drawing your favorite things is the next best thing to buying them. Make little drawings of items on your wish list right now.

148 Draw the cover of your favorite book or magazine.

149 Draw all the houses you have ever lived in, from your childhood home right up to where you live now.

150 Draw your dream house.

151 "Doodles have the power to be anything," says artist Jon Burgerman, known for doodling new bodies for the people sitting opposite him on the train. In the spirit of Burgerman, glue three heads cut from magazines or newspapers to this page and give them wild imaginary bodies.

152 "You can choose your own material, but your style of drawing chooses you." If you find your own style, you will feel more confident in drawing. It's like finding your own voice. Glue a picture or illustration that you like on this page and try to copy it in different styles.

Note what style of drawing feels most natural to you.

CONNECT

LIFE IS ALL ABOUT CONNECTING WITH
WHAT'S AROUND YOU

I met a nice young traveler from Brazil the other day.

He studied psychology, but had taken a year off to figure out some things for himself. He had stumbled on my little neighborhood in the outskirts of Amsterdam and one of my neighbors had invited him to stay with her family because the hostel was fully booked. We were standing outside on a summer evening, the neighborhood kids had just ended a playful water fight, and everybody was happy and cheerful. Some neighbors had brought their after-dinner coffee with them; I was sipping on a glass of wine. When the subject came to our Brazilian visitor, my neighbor said jokingly, "He's here looking for the meaning of life."

"Ah," I replied, laughing. "He's come to the right place. The meaning of life is here; it's us talking about the meaning of life."

I was partly kidding, of course. I don't have a clue what the true meaning is. But I do know what gives my life meaning. And that is connection. Connection with my loved ones around me, but also moments of real connection with my neighbors and other people who happen to cross my path. Those random positive encounters on the street, or a thoughtful gesture from a friend, are full of happiness. I used to think that was just because I'm an extrovert, but recent research shows that everybody craves real connection, even introverts— maybe on different terms, but they crave it nonetheless.

So, the key to happiness is being kind and not only to other people. It's about being kind to yourself and everything that surrounds you. This chapter is bursting with creative and mindful prompts about connection, in the broadest sense of the word, because connection gives everything meaning.

153 Research shows that supportive friends are extremely important to your well-being. Think about how your friends support you. Which friend comes to mind first?

Write about him or her, and how they've supported you.

154 "A stranger is just a friend you haven't met yet," said the American entertainer Will Rogers (1879–1935). Think of someone you've seen around, but haven't met in person. Draw the person and yourself as friends.

155 Online you can find thousands of pictures of heart shapes that people have found in clouds, stones, flowers, and so on. "It's like nature saying I love you," said actress Drew Barrymore, who wrote a book about the phenomenon. Go out on a hunt for heart shapes today. Draw one you find here.

156 We share the planet with millions of other humans, each with their own lives and thoughts, and yet we walk past tens or even hundreds of them each day, making absolutely no connection. Make today the day you smile at everyone you see and don't stop until you get a smile back.

Jot down notes about the experience and how it felt.

NOTES

157 Compassion is an important part of being mindful. Anger and irritation get in the way of feeling good. Realizing that even the most annoying people in your life have good qualities makes a big difference in how you feel about them. Pick one person you have issues with. *Use this space to write about their best traits or the positive side to their annoying habits.*

POSITIVE

NEGATIVE

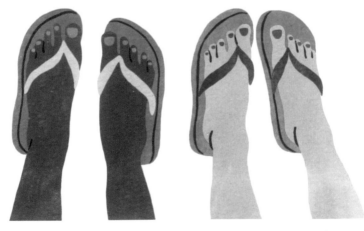

158 Connect with your feet. Your feet take you everywhere; they're working all day long. *Give them a nice massage and take a moment to be aware of them and thankful for the amazing job that they do.*

159

Ask a friend or family member
to draw you and point out the things that
he/she loves about you.

160 Look in your bag or pockets for a ticket to an event that you attended with a friend, like a movie ticket. Paste it here. Who did you go with? How was it? What did you talk about?

161 Love is all around us! Look for small gestures of affection between other people. Keep an eye out for couples holding hands, parents cuddling their children, friends hugging.

Sketch a sweet scene that you saw today.

162 We tend to forget compliments and focus on criticisms; it's just how humans are wired. Researcher John Gottman calculated that in a relationship, no fewer than five positive interactions are needed to turn the mad mojo around following one negative interaction. So, focus on the positive today. Note all the compliments that you receive, from anyone, no matter how small, no matter if it's just a look of appreciation or a hand on your shoulder. *List them here.*

COMPLIMENT   FROM WHOM

1

2

3

4

5

163 Who said friendship bracelets are only for kids? Buy some brightly colored threads and start braiding for a friend. *The little things in life make all the difference.*

164 "People who dare to be vulnerable in relationships are the happiest," says American researcher and writer Brené Brown. Not being ashamed of your weaknesses and not covering them up is the key to real human connection.

What are the weaknesses that you would rather hide from people? When do you feel vulnerable? What people do you feel safe with?

165 What do you remember from the first time you were in love with someone?

166 It's always scary to make the first move, to be the first one to apologize, or to tell someone the truth. Visualize the first step of a social interaction that you dread.

Sketch or describe the situation and what you would say. Sorry

167 When we talk with another person, we mirror each other's facial expressions and body language. In the next meeting with someone you like, notice your mirroring behavior. You might also be able to spot it in other people's interactions with you.

168 The loss of precious connections can be devastating, but we keep our loved ones alive in our hearts and in our memories. Write a postcard to a loved one who has passed away and draw a picture on the front that connects you to each other.

169 In Mongolia, the shamans believe that everything has a soul, even rocks and mountains. Because of that, they treat every little thing with respect.

Look at your surroundings as if everything has a soul and draw the objects that catch your eye.

170 Find an object, an item of clothing, or a picture that makes you think about an event or person from the past. Write down the memories that come to mind.

171 People love helping others most of the time, but asking for help is one of the hardest things to do. In what area would you like help in your life? Write a message reaching out for help. Consider passing it on to someone who might be able to give you what you need.

172 Just because we lose touch with people doesn't mean that we don't think or care about them. Pick up the phone and call someone you've been meaning to reconnect with for some time.

Jot down a nice memory that you share.

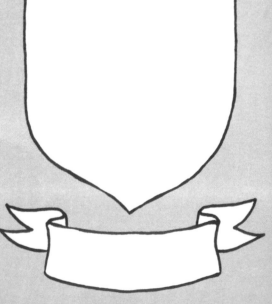

173 A family crest has been the distinctive mark of a family since the Middle Ages; it was used for flags and clothing, and was central to clan identity. Of course, crests are no longer widely used, but why not design your own with symbols that represent your family?

174 Describe your mother's character. How are you like her?

175 Describe your father's character. How are you like him?

176

Draw your grandfather or grandmother in his or her favorite outfit.

177 "Metta" means loving-kindness, friendliness, amity; it's one of the sublime states of being in Buddhism. A metta-meditation is a compassion meditation where you open your heart to others, but also to yourself. Write down some kind thoughts about yourself in these hearts.

Meditate for five minutes on these thoughts.

178 How are you? Connect with your feelings and emotions. Imagine that you had to make a weather report of how you feel right now. What would it say?

Draw little weather report symbols with it.

179 When you make somebody happy, you become happier yourself; in psychology, that's called "empathic joy." Try to tick as many of these boxes with random acts of kindness. In addition to making someone else's day, it might just make you smile.

- [ ] Let someone cut ahead in a line.
- [ ] Help someone with their groceries.
- [ ] Smile at a stranger.
- [ ] Offer directions to a person who looks lost.
- [ ] Offer to give someone a ride.
- [ ] Pick up something a child dropped.
- [ ] Give a heartfelt compliment.

180 Write, draw, and/or illustrate the name of someone you love.

181 Make a cartoon from a social encounter that really made you laugh, using stick figures to represent you and the people with whom you had the interaction. *Write what was said in speech bubbles.*

182 Before photography, people would often give dear friends or family members a locket containing a miniature portrait of themselves. The locket would sometimes contain a lock of hair and be decorated with fine symbols, such as the pansy (in French, *Pensée*, or *pense à moi*, think of me).

Paint a mini portrait of yourself in this locket and add some flowers or symbols.

183 It can be incredibly meaningful to realize that you're part of a bigger picture. Make a mind map about the people in your life. Start with yourself in the middle and go from there to include family and friends. Use colors, arrows, words, and little drawings to note how close you are, who is connected to whom, and what activities you do with them.

Me

SENSES

TURN OFF YOUR AUTOMATIC PILOT

AND LIVE IN THE NOW

Your senses are great helpers for being mindful. What you see, hear, feel, taste, and smell can only be experienced in the now; your senses don't take notice of what's happening in the past or future. Take sounds, for example: what you hear is NOW. The clock ticking, the wind blowing, a car going by. Sounds change constantly and if you listen carefully, you hear that everything has its own sound, even silence. But how often are we really noticing what we experience through our senses?

I used to go through life on automatic pilot, lost in my thoughts, busy worrying or planning or stuck behind a screen. Yes, I used my eyes, but did I really see?

Then one day a mindfulness teacher pointed out that the senses are the best way to get back in the now. And by paying more attention to them, instead of just taking them for granted, we experience life more fully as a bonus. He told me, "If you're mindful enough to notice all the sounds, colors, smells, and other sensations that are around us all the time, life gets more interesting straight away."

So now, whenever I'm lost in my thoughts and feel disconnected from the present moment, I focus on my senses. How does the breeze feel on my face? I really pay attention and sometimes I can even feel the vibrations of sounds. I notice how colors change constantly because of the movement of the sun across the sky; it's beautiful! In these mindful moments, I slowly start to see my surroundings for what they really are. It's as though I'm opening up and my head is clearing. Even if it's only for that moment, I feel like I'm connected with the present and I have more clarity for the next moment to come— at least until my phone rings.

184 Go outside and focus on birds singing. Try to capture the way a bird sings in a drawing, with lines flicking up and down, and long and short spaces between; let the sounds steer your hand.

185 Write down all the sounds that you can currently hear.

Don't stop until you have at least five.

186 Eating is a great opportunity to practice mindfulness. We stop what we're doing to satisfy our hunger and at the same time we can connect to our senses. When eating, take time to notice the different flavors in each mouthful. Close your eyes as you chew to focus on the taste.

187 Each of the senses has a distinct purpose and method of delivering messages to our brains. Touch, for example, is less precise in some ways than sight. Explore this by picking up a mystery object and trying to draw it without looking at it; use only your sense of touch as guidance.

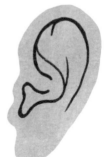

188 Imagine that the sounds you're hearing are produced by colors instead of vibrations. Draw the colors entering your ears right now.

189 Research shows that the aromatic compounds of nature contribute to the well-being that we experience when spending time in the great outdoors. Go outside to investigate the smell of trees. Do you smell the difference between a young tree and an old tree?

Jot down your notes here.

190 We are used to using maps, in visual terms, to find our way from place to place, but we can also represent the other senses in this way. Make a mini map of your neighborhood with descriptions of the scents and sounds that can be found there daily.

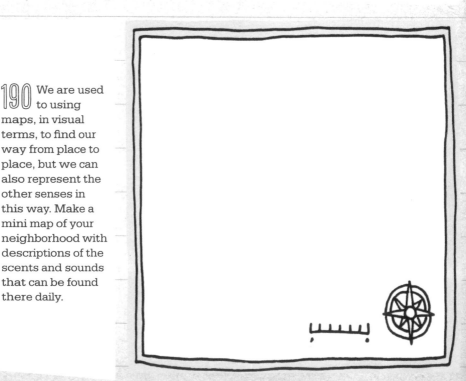

191 When is a tree just plain brown and green? Is it ever? At sunset, the trunks can look deep purple and the leaves as if they're made from gold; in the moonlight, the leaves turn to majestic blue. Take your crayons, find a tree and really look at it. Wait until you can see past your preconceptions and automatic gaze, and draw it in the actual colors that you can see right now.

192 Our skin is always touching something: the air around us, our clothes, the chair. Most of the time we are totally unaware of it. Take a moment to tune in to what you are feeling. What's happening to your skin right now?

Describe the textures, temperatures, and sensations.

193 Take a walk, focusing only on the feelings in your feet. Notice how they touch and leave the ground.

Sketch the movement of your feet.

SENSES

194 Look around you and notice the shadows cast by the objects you can see.

Draw an object and its shadow on this page.

195 Inhale deeply. What can you smell right now? Try to focus on a different scent with every inhalation.

Draw the sources of the smells on this page.

196 Recall an activity where you were completely in the moment; for example, when you were swimming, cycling, or taking a bath. Note how you felt by describing only what your senses experienced.

197 What are your three favorite scents? *Draw them here.*

198 If you look closely, you see that everything has its own color. Count the different shades that you can see right in front of you now.

199

Imagine you are color blind. What color would you miss most? Write it here. Be as specific as possible. What shade of color is it? Where do you find it normally? What would life be like without it?

....
....
....
....
....
....
....
....
....

200 Objects can lose their familiarity and take on new forms when we explore them with senses other than sight. Find a leaf, close your eyes and explore it with your fingertips. Note three things about it from your experiences with touch.

One	Two	Three

201 The fine ridges on our fingers, arranged in loops, whorls, and arches, are unique to us. That is, of course, the reason fingerprints are used to identify individuals. A recent study explained that the reason we have fingerprints in the first place is that it enhances our sense of touch. Print one of your fingertips here.

202 Shower in the dark! Write about your experience. Before you start, make sure everything is where it normally is in your shower, so you know you'll feel safe.

203 When we hear a noise, we tend to name it: a car passing, water running, a child laughing. Instead of naming a sound, try describing it, allowing you to concentrate on the experience of simply hearing it.

204 Consider a loaf of bread using all your senses. You may be familiar with how it smells and tastes, but look at the shape it's developed while baking, tap the loaf to hear what sound it makes, and feel the texture of the inside compared to the crust.

205 It has always been thought that dogs have a better sense of smell than humans. But humans also have a very developed smelling sense; we just don't focus that much on what we smell. Try to experience the world through the nose of a dog; draw your street and use different crayons to mark the different scented trails and marks. What and where are the smells that we don't normally notice?

206
Draw your
own nose,
the nose
of a friend,
and of
a family
member.

Friend

Family

You

207 Walk around with bare feet and feel the texture of the earth, stones, or grass beneath them. *Jot down how it felt.*

208 What was the first thing you heard this morning?

Make a quick drawing.

209 Make intuitive drawings of the sounds that you associate with these words.

Morning

Friends

Happiness

Vacation

Love

210 Spray your favorite perfume on this page and describe the smell.

211 We don't register everything we see around us all at once; our minds fill in a lot automatically. This is a big help—we would go crazy otherwise—but it's also the reason we miss a lot. Look at your surroundings mindfully.

Notice at least three things that you haven't noticed before and write them down here.

One	*Two*	*Three*

212 The fact that smells can bring you back to a memory in a heartbeat is a phenomenon called olfactory-evoked recall: the recollection of a past memory stimulated by an aroma.

Think of three important smells from your childhood and allow yourself to drift back to where they want to take you. Write down what you remember.

213 Delight your fingertips by collecting different textures of paper and fabric and gluing them onto these pages.

WRITE

WHY DO WE WRITE?

WHAT DOES IT DO FOR US?

That can maybe best be explained by the words of famous writers. "We write to taste life twice, in the moment and in retrospect," said French-born novelist **Anaïs Nin** (1903–1977), most famous for her journals. We write to remember and to cherish special moments in our life. But we also write to clear our heads and make room for new thoughts. Some even consider writing therapeutic. A great example is **Anne Frank** (1929–1945), who wrote in her world-famous diary: "I can shake off everything as I write; my sorrows disappear, my courage is reborn." Some people write simply because they have to.

"There is no greater agony than bearing an untold story inside you," said American writer and poet **Maya Angelou** (1928–2014).

There's something about the act of writing that connects with our deepest thoughts. Sometimes when I write, it's like my pen takes over. That's just a wonderful feeling. Thoughts make it to the page, but also fantasies and storylines that simmer deep inside. We tap into our secret wishes and dreams. Drawing letters and words is also a fun and relaxing way to create something beautiful.

This chapter is a mix of writing assignments and prompts about the simple fun of creating words and letters. Find a nice place to sit, pick up your favorite pen, and give it some time. To end with the words of the legendary American writer **Sylvia Plath** (1932–1963): "Everything in life is writable about if you have the outgoing guts to do it, and the imagination to improvise. The worst enemy to creativity is self-doubt."

214 "Don't tell me the moon is shining; show me the glint of light on broken glass," said the Russian playwright Anton Chekhov (1860–1904). Basically, don't tell, but show. Describe your childhood room and try to show it in as much detail as possible: smells, colors, sounds, wall posters.

215 Write a poem about your day without using rhyming words. Play with alliteration and rhythm instead.

216 Words have the power to give people a good feeling without them knowing why. What are the words that you associate with happiness? Write as many as you can think of in the circle around the word "happiness". Then write words that you associate with those words in the area outside the circle.

HAPPINESS

217 Writing about what you're grateful for in life has a positive effect on your well-being, research has shown. But writing about your sorrow also has a therapeutic effect. Writing basically makes you feel good, even when it's about things that hurt. Write about a painful moment in your life.

218 Describe a moment you hope to celebrate in the future.

219 If you could spend the day doing absolutely anything with anyone, who would you spend it with and what would you do? Write about that day.

The only limit is your imagination.

220 Go rummaging in a flea market or a second-hand shop for treasure. Select an item that speaks to you—an old teddy bear, an item of clothing, a book, a pot—and fantasize about the previous owner.

Who was he or she? What was their story?

221 Positive emotions open you up "like a flower opening up to the sun," says the American researcher Barbara Fredrickson. So, it helps to think of the good things in your life if you want to embark on a creative task. Write down all that's positive in your life right now.

222 Design the front cover of a book you might write one day.

223 Learning from the writers who came before you is a great way to motivate yourself.

Which writers inspire you? Make a list.

224 Go through your bookcase and find some of your favorite books. Flip through them while focusing on the narrative style. For example, is it written in the past tense? Is it a first-person story? Is there more than one storyline? Make notes here about your findings and what you like about the different styles.

225 Write a letter to your younger self.

226 What is the best advice you've ever been given? By whom?

227 Put on some of your favorite energizing music and turn your phone off. Move your hand to the music and write down everything that comes to mind.

Don't stop until the page is full.

228 The moon has been a romantic inspiration from the moment people started telling stories.

Draw the moon you see tonight and write a little poem or story as an ode to it.

229 Almost every family harbors a story that could be made into a book: adventures of pioneering great-grandparents; the uncle who chose a different path; the love story of your parents. What is the story in your family?

Write down what you know or ask a family member.

230
LOVE LETTER

We are surrounded by beautifully presented words and lettering —in design books, on shop windows, in advertisements. Take pictures and try to replicate them.

Make this page your playground for sketches of the interesting fonts that you find.

231
Researchers have found that people are better able to remember handwritten notes than notes typed on a computer. You absorb your notes differently and better. Watch a documentary you've had on your to-see list for a while and scribble down notes and quotes here that you find interesting.

232 Illustrate the first letter of your name in the most beautiful, colorful way possible, just as you would find letters in old fairy tale books.

233 Write a story about your day, playing around with font size, writing style, bold, italic, capital and lower case letters.

Notice what it does for your story and your creative thinking when you write this way.

234

Cut out a few paper squares, fold them in the middle, and staple them together to make a tiny booklet. Create a cover and a little story with drawings inside.

235 Write about your first day of high school.

236 Our life experiences are a great source for writing. Look back over your past and bring memories to life on the page. Write about the most embarrassing moment you can remember.

Then write about a moment you're proud of.

237 A wonderful part of writing is that anything is possible; we can visit places we don't have access to in real life—including the past. Imagine you had the option to live in a different era. Write about the period you would choose and what you would do.

238 Flip through an old dictionary and search for three intriguing words you've never used before. Write the words in the boxes and create a short story using them.

Word 1	Word 2	Word 3

239 Write about your day as if you were a butterfly.

240 Writing a haiku, a type of Japanese poem, is an extremely meditative and fulfilling way to play with words. Because haikus are always composed the same way, you don't have to invent a composition structure yourself. The first of the three lines has five syllables, the second line has seven syllables, and the last has five syllables again.

Write a haiku about your favorite season.

241 Writing is perfect for getting to know yourself and to reflect on your life. Start writing as soon as you read these questions. Don't overthink the answers. Let your pen answer for you.

★ *If you could change anything about the way you were brought up, what would you change?*

★ *What would you do differently if you could live your teenage years again?*

★ *When are you the happiest?*

242 Create a small timeline of your life up to now. What were the most important events?

243 Where do you feel most inspired to write? In a quiet room? At a windowsill in your house? In a bustling café with familiar background noises? Describe or draw your favorite spot.

Point out the elements you specifically like about it.

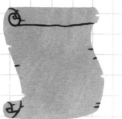

244 Handwrite your favorite quote or life motto. Use the whole spread to try out different styles.

CREATE

GIVE YOUR CREATIVE

STREAK FREE REIN

AND BOOST YOUR POSITIVITY!

Even though I almost never finish anything and two of my cupboards are bursting out of their joints with tools and materials, crafting never bores me. Every time I take a moment to create something, I feel a little bit lighter. Doesn't matter if it's something small and insignificant, or even if the outcome is just plain ugly; the act in itself does something for me.

So, I wasn't surprised to read that research at the University of Otago in New Zealand showed that doing something creative not only has a positive effect on the same day, but it lasts even into the next day. Doing creative things makes people feel *"flourishing"* (the exact word used in the report). Everyday creativity, the researchers concluded, is a way to "cultivate positive psychological functioning." Well, it certainly helps my positive psychological functioning. As soon as we sit down and make time to create something, it's like going to a happy place. Creating makes us feel joyful and energized, and the good news is that we can all benefit from it. Some people might be more gifted than others, but creativity is a universal human trait and something we can improve by practicing. Our brains are wired to make connections, to invent new things, and to think of creative solutions to problems, because our ancestors simply needed those skills to survive. No wonder it gives us a positive feeling; we're meant to create. It's in our nature.

So, leave the self-doubt; you don't need it. Leave your ambition too; it will block your flow. Search for something you like doing: try different things, have fun shopping for art supplies or look around you for suitable material—anything can be used to create. And most of all, have fun!

245 One of the simplest and most useful things to create is a bookmark. Start by making your own from a piece of cardboard and use it in this book! You can paint it, glue bits of scrap paper or fabric on it, cut shapes out of it, and make a hole at one end for ribbon or a tassel.

246 Create a decorative design for this tote bag.

247 Place flat but textured objects under the page and trace over them with colored pencils to make a pattern or picture. Try buttons, textured cardboard, orange peel, plastic packaging —anything that feels interesting.

248 Creating anything is such an immersive experience that the time simply flies by. Can you remember a moment when you completely lost track of time while creating something?

Describe that moment.

249 Draw around your hand and give the fingers faces and accessories. *Are they friends? Family? A sports team?*

250 Make your wish list of art supplies you'd like to have or try out.

251 Use watercolor paint to make random blobs on this page. When you're done, use a black fine-point pen or India ink to make the blobs into something else, like an animal or an object.

252 Go big! Use the biggest paintbrush you can find in your house and paint a self-portrait. That way, you can't fuss about the details.

253 Turning something old into something new always produces exciting results. Try this by cutting out part of an old picture, pasting it here, and drawing a new scene around it.

254 Create a logo for yourself as if you were a company or a product. Look at the logos all around you—on food packaging and magazines, letters, and shopfronts —for inspiration. Carefully consider the type of lettering and the colors you would use.

255 During the period when Picasso was suffering from depression (1901–4), he only used shades of blue and blue-green to create his paintings. The Blue Period was followed by his Rose Period, when things started to get better and he fell in love. What colors represent the mood you are in now?

Use shades of that color to draw something here.

256 Art materials can be found everywhere, even in the everyday things that people throw away. Bottle caps are a great example of this; people drop bottle caps everywhere. Collect as many as you can, sort them by color, and take a picture or draw them.

257 Fill this page with colorful balloons cut from different types of paper.

Add patterns or designs to these
items of children's clothing.

259 Create a pattern using colored masking tape or washi tape.

260 Take a closer look at the shapes you see every day. *Draw an outline around small household objects and see what you can create.*

261 Mix paint to create new shades of color. Have fun inventing names for the colors you created.

262 Blend paint colors to match these ideas:

Spring love

Summer breeze

Into the wild

Grandma's house

263 Potato stamping! Cut a potato in half. Carve a simple shape out of each half of the potato and use it as a stamp *(carve away what you don't want to see)*. Create a pattern on this page with the two shapes and different colors of paint.

264 Design a collection of four postage stamps using the theme "water."

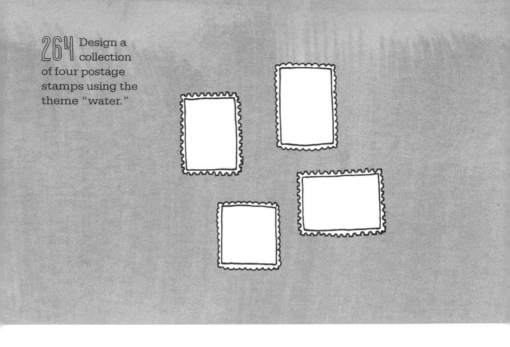

265 Go small! Create a miniature town by cutting out mini buildings, trees, and cars. The smaller the better.

Use tweezers to hold them and help you glue them into place.

266

Maybe you remember this
from when you were a kid: fold a
piece of paper a couple of times, cut
little shapes in it and when you unfold
the piece of paper again, you've
created a pattern. Have some fun
experimenting with different
ways of cutting the paper.

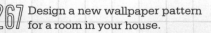

267 Design a new wallpaper pattern
for a room in your house.

268 If you're looking for inspiration, it helps to give yourself restrictions. Restrictions force your brain to look for creative solutions and are proven to challenge you to think outside the box.

For example, by drawing in this frame, you are likely to create something different than if you used the whole page.

269 Create a picture using just two colored pencils— but keep switching between them. Use each color for just five seconds, then swap to the other and carry on where you left off, whatever part of the picture you're on.

270 You don't have to start each drawing or painting from scratch; you can use a lightbox to transfer earlier drawings or photographs of landscapes or buildings, for example. To create your own temporary lightbox, tape the image you want to transfer onto a window with masking tape, tape white paper over it, and trace the most important lines you see shining through the paper. Transfer the picture onto this page and use it as a background for a drawing.

271 Create a painting of a plant using different layers to give the painting more depth. Start with a vague, transparent blob as the background and use thicker paint and more details as you work your way to the front leaves.

Mix different materials, like crayons, watercolors, and acrylic paints.

272 Take inspiration from great artists of the past. Which artists do you find inspiring?

Look through some art books and make a list of your top five.

1

2

3

4

5

273 Abstract art is all about stripping images down to simple lines, shapes, and colors. Create an abstract drawing of a scene from a bird's view, like a landscape or an outside terrace from a restaurant.

Leave out all the realistic detail and use bright colors and simple shapes.

274 Schedule an art date with a friend or fly solo and go to a museum, gallery, or exhibition.

275 Use a cut-out piece from a newspaper as a background for a painting. *Allow the content of the article to inspire your artwork.*

EXPLORE

THE MORE YOU EXPLORE, THE MORE YOU WILL DISCOVER

One day, at the age of eleven, on my daily route to school, I discovered a beautiful community garden. I'd never seen it before, but I'd taken a little detour to avoid some annoying boys I saw coming my way. I will never forget how I felt when I discovered this magical garden, full of flowers and bees and butterflies and plants I had never seen before. From that day on, I visited that garden all the time; it became my secret hiding place.

People are creatures of habit. We are wired to resist changes and we avoid stepping out of our comfort zones. And before we know it, we're always walking along the same paths and visiting the same places. But the real magic happens when we leave our comfort zones and try new things. That's why we should never stop exploring. Life is just too short to always be doing the same thing.

This chapter is about exploring in the broadest sense of the word: exploring what you like and don't like, where you want to go and what you want to do. You don't have to go far; some discoveries are just around the corner. When exploring, your world gets bigger and your creativity will be activated by it. It wakes you up, sheds new light on old habits and most of all, helps you build new memories.

Even now, thirty years later, when I have my own four square yards in a community garden, I can still recall that enchanted moment of discovery as if it was yesterday. Maybe my love for gardens and flowers started there, at that moment. We'll never know. But I wholeheartedly agree with what Carson the butler said in *Downton Abbey*:

"The business of life is the acquisition of memories. In the end, that's all there is."

276 Make a list of five countries and/or cities you would like to explore. Leave the sixth one open *(see the next prompt)*.

1. ....

2. ....

3. ....

4. ....

5. ....

6. ....

277 Let serendipity decide your sixth choice. If you have a globe, spin it, point at it with your eyes closed and add the result to your list.

278 To obtain "genuinely chance impressions of cities and countries, the traveller and wanderer should trust neither their own choice of road, nor the guide's choice, nor the map." So writes Stephen Graham in his book *The Gentle Art of Tramping* (1927), a well-known book among modern explorers. One of Graham's recommendations is to discover an area by going on a "zigzag walk": take the first turn to the left, then the first to the right, then the first to the left again, and so on.

Try the zigzag walk today and make notes about the experience.

NOTES

....

....

....

....

....

....

....

279 Go to the supermarket and look for something you've never eaten before, something exotic. This is even more fun if you're in another country. Take it home and try it.

Draw it here.

What is it?

....

Taste?

....

Origin?

....

280 Driving a camper van is like being on vacation from the start. If you don't own one, try the next best thing: draw one. It's like creating a little vacation in your mind.

Where would you go first?

281 There is so much to discover near our own homes. When going to the store, instead of going straight from A to B, take a little detour through an area you don't know well. Stop somewhere and take a look around. *What do you see?*

282

What do you know about the area you live in?
Find out the answers to the following questions.

What's the name of your street and why is it named that way?

What's the name of your town, city, or village and where does this name come from?

What's your country called in different languages?

What does the name of your country mean?

283 Play with binoculars! Take them with you when going on a walk and find something to climb on to get a good view.

Explore something in the distance and draw it here.

284 Explore the hidden treasures in your house. Go through your junk drawer (everybody has one). Search for something that makes you smile because of a nice memory: a postcard, a used ticket, a little souvenir.

Draw it here and jot down the memory.

285 A fine way to wander without a goal is to go on a "heart-walk" where you let yourself be guided by symbols. Whenever you see a heart shape *(or another interesting shape)* in a tree, or in a puddle, go that way.

286 Find the strangest object you can today and explore it.

287 "If there were no mystery left to explore, life would get rather dull, wouldn't it?" said the American screenwriter Sidney Buchman (1902–1975).

Note down your thoughts on a theory or idea that you find mysterious.

288 Our brain doesn't have a watch; it measures time on the basis of new incentives and experiences. If there is a lot to process, time seems to last longer. That's why a three-day trip can feel like you've been away for a week. So, basically, adventures prolong your life.

Make a bucket list of grand adventures.

289 Let your friends be your guides in exploring new things. Ask them what you should definitely try out. It could be anything, from a movie or sport, to learning to play an instrument. *Make plans to try them.*

290 Outside of your comfort zone is where most of the magic happens. It's where you find unexpected beauty; it's where you learn that you are capable of more than you think; it's where you meet new people; it's where you create amazing things and great stories to tell. *Recall a moment when you were completely out of your comfort zone and something beautiful happened.*

291 The fear of failing is what holds us back from trying new things. The only way to overcome the fear of failing is to deliberately pursue experiences where we are bound to fail. So that's a paradox. It might help to realize that failure is extremely valuable to the creative process. The Irish playwright and novelist Samuel Beckett (1906–1989) even believed that failing was an essential part of the artist's work. "Ever tried. Ever failed. No matter. Try again. Fail again. Fail better." *When were you, or are you, afraid of failing?*

292

Meditate somewhere new.

293 Try using the "wrong" colors in a drawing. If it makes you feel uncomfortable, you're on the right track.

294 Learning new things is like exploring new worlds. And every fresh thing you learn opens a new horizon, showing you new places to go. Jot down five fields you would like to know more about or even study.

1
2
3
4
5

295 Learn a useful sentence in a foreign language. Write it down, spelled correctly and phonetically, and make drawings to help you remember it.

Practice until you know it by heart.

296 What are you passionate about? You don't have to quit your day job to follow your passion. Just schedule time for it. Think of any hobbies or side projects you want to explore and draw or write about them here.

297 Ponder this question for a while: How do I live life as fully as possible?

EXPLORE

298

Explore your dreams. *Make a colorful drawing of a fantasy.*

299 Draw a wilderness that you would like to visit.

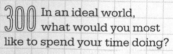

300 In an ideal world, what would you most like to spend your time doing?

Draw or jot down some activities you would like to pursue.

301 Spend time exploring new music. Ask friends, search online, find a record store. Try to add three new names to your list of favorite groups or musicians.

302 Just before bedtime, instead of checking social media or your e-mails, take a walk outside. Explore your neighborhood at night, peek inside the lighted houses, note the dog walkers on their last round, listen to evening birds singing.

Make notes or draw sketches inspired by your nighttime walk.

303 Write a story in a hundred words about your first vacation without your parents.

What did you discover?

304 Make a collage of your dream vacation. Print inspiring pictures you find online, then mix them with pictures from magazines and your own vacation photos.

EAT

FOOD NOURISHES YOUR BODY

AND YOUR MIND

"What's for dinner?"
The daily "what-are-we-going-to-eat?"
hassle can be so annoying, deciding what
to eat and shopping for groceries. But
food can be so much more than that. It *is*
so much more than that. Food connects
people, food triggers the senses, food
inspires emotions: You can put so much
of your creativity into it.

If you think about it, simply because
you have to eat every single day, food
is a perfect daily outlet for creativity
and practice for embracing the now.
Appreciating where the food you eat is
coming from, paying attention to the

process of cooking, even setting the table—all help to make eating a more mindful, creative experience. It would be a shame to miss out on that, wouldn't it?

One way to enjoy the process of cooking is simply to take more time with it. Slow down; don't rush it. As **Michael Pollan**, author of *Cooked* and *Food Rules*, says, *"When chopping onions, just chop onions."* The moment you start to see cooking as a way of taking time for yourself, instead of seeing it as a daily hurdle, it turns into something far more fun and relaxing. It's your time, plus the result even makes other people happy.

Also, as a side benefit, you might just start to eat more healthily, cooking with more fresh products and letting go of the rushed meal in front of the TV. So, forget about diets, counting calories, and food hypes. Look at the colors of food instead. Draw it, smell it, play with it, decorate it and, most importantly, eat!

305 Thinking back to our childhood is a great way to remind us of our true passions and unearth the playful selves that can get lost under layers of adulthood and responsibility. What was your favorite meal when you were a child?

Write down one memory of having that meal.

306 Look for fruit stickers and stick one here. Or make a pattern using lots of them.

307 SOUP: IT'S GREAT!
You can put everything in it and you just have to stir. You can invite everyone last minute because you can easily make more. It's comforting, it's hot, it's easy to eat, and it's full of nutrition. Describe your favorite soup.

308 The journeys taken by ingredients to reach our cooking pots are often mind-blowing adventures, so be mindful of where your food comes from.

Choose one thing you ate today and try to answer these questions:

Where did it come from/grow?

Who was in contact with it before you?

How did it get to your town?

How did it get to your kitchen?

309 The wonder of honey bees! To tell other bees where they can find good foraging places, honey bees perform the "waggle dance," which tells other bees the distance and direction. It's a movement in a figure-eight shape.

Draw some bees around this beehive.

310 What did you eat today?
Make a list.

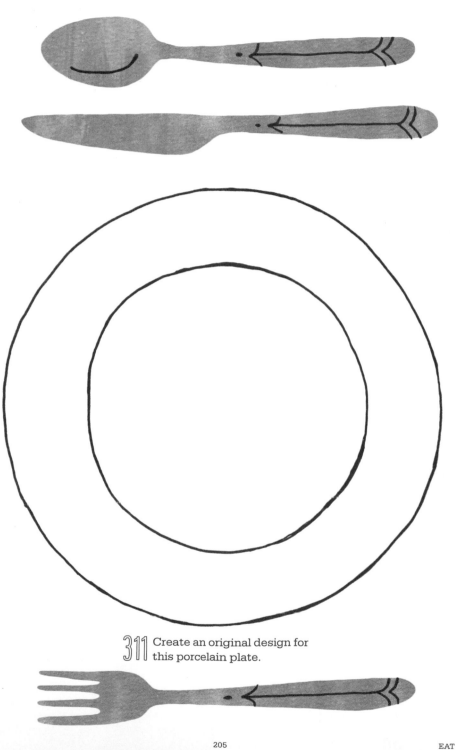

311 Create an original design for this porcelain plate.

EAT

312 When humans started to cook with fire, they also had a focal point around which to gather and talk. Recall a campfire moment when you had a deep conversation with someone.

Jot down your memory, what you talked about and what you ate.

313 Try something new. Choose three foods you've never eaten, or think you don't like, and write down how they taste.

One

Two

Three

314 Special treats can link to happy childhood memories. Think of a sweet treat that made you happy as a child.

Draw it and tap into your memory by describing it.

315 We are so used to buying our food from stores that we sometimes forget the ways people used to collect food themselves. We still could; there are so many wild flowers and weeds that you can eat. The young leaves of a dandelion; the flowers of a purple violet; the flowers of the nasturtium; the leaves of ground elders. Investigate the edible weeds and flowers that grow in your neighborhood and make a flower salad. Double-check online to make sure what you find is edible.

Don't pick anything that is chemically treated or found next to a busy road.

316

There is beauty in everything, even in food packaging.

Draw a selection of bottles, cans, and cartons from your kitchen cabinet.

317 Make a sketch of the person behind the counter of your favorite café or local store you visit regularly.

318 A common practice in a mindfulness course is the mindful eating of a raisin. It draws all the attention to the senses and, more importantly, to the moment. Take one raisin out of a box. Before you eat it, squeeze it softly next to your ear; what do you hear? Smell it, look at it closely, notice how your mouth automatically produces saliva. And lastly, taste it before you eat it.

Make notes on your experience.

EAT

319 When you feel bad about something, drinking a hot beverage immediately lifts your spirits a little bit. Researchers found that drinking something warm can even make a person friendlier.

Put the kettle on and draw your tea or coffee cup.

320 What did your grandmother or grandfather used to cook for you?

321 Put a little glue in the circles on this page. Fill each circle with a different herb or spice. Note next to each what kind of spices you have used and any memories that surface.

EAT

322 Fill this cabinet with a range of decorative pottery.

323 Freshly made infusions with blossoms and herbs are not just a treat for your palate, but for all your senses. Discover what grows in your own backyard or neighborhood, like red clover, mint, or violets, and maybe add some orange peel to experiment with your own aromatic tea break.

Keep note of where you found your ingredients and the perfect combinations of your brew.

324 Lunch is so often squeezed into our busy schedules that some people no longer even sit down for it, eating a sandwich or a bagel on the run while doing a hundred other things at once. Not today! Describe your favorite lunch and make the description as mouth-watering and enticing as possible. Then treat yourself by bringing it to life.

325 Draw your favorite ingredients.

EAT

326 A beautifully decorated table elevates the whole experience of eating. If you set the table and pay attention to the decorations, people—even children—perceive eating as more enjoyable and better tasting.

Make a sketch with notes for a fantasy table setting, perhaps themed, letting your imagination go wild.

327 Dinner setting idea: Cut four paper strips and paint them decoratively. Wrap them around four sets of cutlery or a cotton napkin, and place them next to the plates.

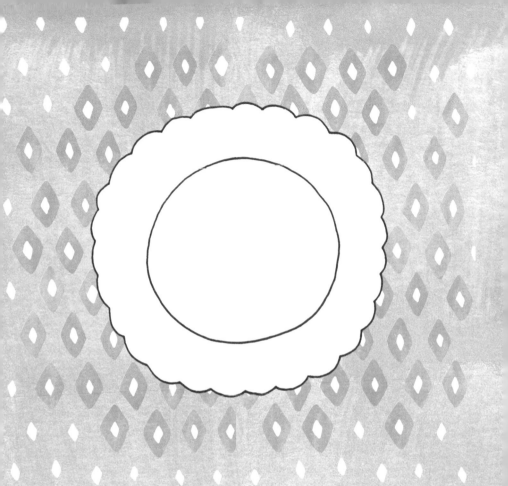

328 Some artists have chosen food as their medium of choice. They make beautiful "paintings" on plates, using simple ingredients, like cucumbers, radishes, cheese, and so on. The basic rule is that it should still be edible afterward. Check out "food art" postings online for inspiration.

Make a sketch of your own food-art masterpiece on this plate and note which food you would use for what.

329 How do you like your eggs? *Draw the answer.*

330 Eat something with an awareness of what it does for your body and make notes about your experience. Is it refreshing? Does it give you energy, fill you up, or feel as if it's giving you a nutritional boost?

331 Collect colorful wrappers from candies and chocolates. *Paste or draw them here.*

332 There is nothing like the color and flavor of a cocktail to transport you to a sandy paradise or a chic metropolis. Invent a new cocktail with all the ingredients you love, give it a groovy name and see where it takes you.

Name:

Ingredients:

333 Imagine you were about to eat the last breakfast you could ever eat in your life.

What would you choose?

334 Imagine you are organizing a tea party in a blossoming garden.

Draw the invitation and create your dream guestlist.

DO NOTHING

JUST BEING INSTEAD OF DOING

IS GOOD FOR OUR BRAIN

Doing nothing is an essential part of creativity. Even **Albert Einstein** said, *"Creativity is the residue of wasted time."* Those moments of non-focus, in a relaxed state, are when our brains make unexpected connections, when things start to fall into place, when you see the world as a whole and not just the part you are focusing on. Just think about the moments when you had a great breakthrough or idea while showering.

What Einstein figured out through his own experience has been proven by neuroscientific research in recent years. Creative leaps are far more likely to happen when the mind is at rest. But doing nothing from time to time is not only important for your creativity; it's so much more. It's those moments of non-focus, of daydreaming, when your brain resets and recharges, researchers found. Workers who take time off are even more productive than workers who don't, so taking a break at lunchtime to do nothing could actually improve your work.

So, good news: we need to stop being efficient all the time and start wasting time! We need to create "white spaces," offline moments to daydream, stroll, take a nap, or—when you're really going for it—to meditate. Don't grab your phone the minute boredom kicks in. Boredom turns into something more interesting if you dare to wait it out a little. Embrace the emptiness; if you're kind to it, it will embrace you back.

336 Put the kettle on to make tea. Don't fill the waiting time with other things. Just wait for the water to boil and think about what's happening with the water. Consider how this exercise differs from your everyday approach as you draw steam coming from this kettle.

335 Scheduling time to do nothing is easier if you have a clearer view of what you spend (or waste!) your time on. Estimate how long you spend on every element of your life— friends, family, phone, a hobby, commuting, running errands, work—and use the pie chart to illustrate the balance of your life.

337 Although we might think that social media relaxes us, our brains are constantly activated by it, leaving us more tired in the end. Think of a plan to create "white spaces" in your life—places and times without electronic devices to distract you.

Note three possible white spaces:

2

1

3

338 It's healthy for your brain to daydream; it recharges it. Fill these clouds with colorful daydreams and dreamy words.

339 In the late 1990s, American neurologist Marcus Raichle discovered that boredom is an extremely valuable state of mind, in which a mixture of thoughts and incentives is on a gentle simmer. Remember the last time you were bored. Describe the situation and your reaction.

340 Take a critical look at the appointments in your schedule. The value you attach to some activities may have changed over the years, because YOU changed. What hobbies or social events do you enjoy less than you did when you started them? What new events do you now enjoy?

341 Meditate for at least five minutes. Tip to help you focus: notice the difference between air coming in and air going out. *Note your findings.*

342 Doing nothing can also mean accepting a situation as it is and not trying to change it. Think of three things in your life that you want to change, but can't at the moment.

Can you let them go?

343 It's almost impossible to tame your thoughts; they are all over the place, like jumping rabbits. But that's not the point of meditating. The point is not to try to make the rabbits sit still, but simply to observe that they are there.

Draw some rabbits and maybe give them some thoughts too.

DO NOTHING

344 Napping is good! In the daytime, it's best if you set the alarm for twenty minutes; it's the most refreshing period and it won't interfere with your nighttime sleep.

Draw a hammock between these trees to take a nap in.

345 Breathe in for four seconds, then out for four seconds. While breathing in, draw four circles; while breathing out, change them into smileys.

Repeat a few breathing cycles until this space is full.

346 Ground yourself in this mountain meditation. Sit in a comfortable position and close your eyes. Imagine yourself as a mountain, your thoughts as clouds passing by, sounds and feelings as the cars, people, and animals walking on or at the foot of the mountain, leaving it unchanged.

Draw them on or around this mountain afterward.

347 Instead of a to-do list, make a to-don't list for today. Think of things you normally do despite your feelings about them, things that are just annoying, or maybe not that important. Add them to your to-don't list and simply don't do them today.

Indulge yourself!

To Don't

348 Schedule in some free time this week and treat it like an important meeting. Make it official by setting an alarm on your phone to remind you it's time.

Also NOT Doing

NOPE

349 Imagine your breath as waves rolling to and from the seashore. Draw the waves that fit your breathing right now. *Are they wild or calm?*

350 To muse is to be completely absorbed in thought, contemplating, reflecting. Spend some time musing when evening falls. Don't turn on the lights yet, while the end of the day is still shimmering.

Jot down your musings.

351 It's estimated that of all the thoughts we have in one day (and that's a lot), only 20 percent are new. Take a critical look at your thoughts and figure out which ones you are repeating over and over.

Write some here.

352 Lying in the grass, look at the clouds and see animals and objects in the drifting fluff. You may remember doing this as a child, but when was the last time you took time out of your day to simply look up?

Draw clouds in different shapes and add the elements you see to them.

353 The unsettled, restless, inconstant, confused, indecisive, uncontrollable train of thoughts that we all normally have in our heads is called the "Monkey Mind" by Buddhists. If certain thoughts bother you, talk to your monkey mind—engaging in conversation with our fears or concerns is a great way of reducing them.

354 Some activities can clear your head like nothing else. When do you feel most relaxed?

Jot down your three most relaxing activities.

1

2

3

355 Draw a palm tree. *Imagine yourself under it.*

DO NOTHING

356 We often say "Yes" to things before we think them through, usually to please others. But then our days are filled with doing things that we don't really want to do. If you have problems saying "No," these steps will make it easier. *Add an example for each one and how you can use it.*

1. Buy yourself time by saying, "I'll get back to you."

....

....

2. Say "No," but suggest an alternative.

....

....

3. Stick to your "No" and keep repeating your message.

....

....

357

Everything changes, even when you do nothing at all. That can be a refreshing thought, to know the world turns without you. Sit down in a green area and take a minute to realize that everything around you is slowly growing and changing.

358 When you're doing nothing and your mind is calm, you start noticing more of the beauty around you. The magic of sunbeams, for example: how they enter a room through the gaps in the curtains, how they find their way through the leaves of a tree, how they make rainbows in droplets of water.

Draw or describe a situation when you were enchanted by sunbeams.

360 Anapana is a meditation on the natural breath entering and leaving the body. Sit comfortably in any posture that suits you, keep your back and neck straight, keep your eyes gently closed, breathe through your nose, and focus your entire attention on the area at the entrance of the nostrils.

As you spend time in this meditation, pay attention to every breath going in and every breath going out.

359 Although we often strive for it, it is impossible to be happy all the time and sad days are okay; chasing happiness every moment stresses us out. Pay attention to the sadness that's inside you right now.

Jot down some notes about it.

Plant a seed in a pot. Water it every day. Watch it grow. Note the seed date and the growth date.

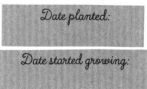

Date planted:

Date started growing:

DO NOTHING

362 Draw a dreamy forest house or log cabin where you could go for an offline retreat. Imagine what you would do there, like writing a book or just hanging out and contemplating your life.

363 Neuroscientists have discovered that multitasking doesn't really exist; we are only ever sequential-tasking, switching from one task to the other and tiring our brain along the way. We try to be more efficient, but in fact we're not. Write down what tasks you are always combining. Try slowing down your pace, one thing at a time. Experiment with committing to the task you're completing before moving to the next.

364 Do nothing for two minutes.

365 Describe and draw your favorite relaxing spots. Mix them with cuttings and clippings from magazines.

Fill these two pages with pictures that help you relax and stay calm.

FURTHER READING

The prompts in this book are mostly based on scientific publications and books. My everlasting gratitude goes out to the researchers and writers of the following works. They have helped me on my quest for well-being and living in the now and I highly recommend checking them out.

ARTICLES

"Experiencing Physical Warmth Promotes Interpersonal Warmth" by John A Bargh and Lawrence E. Williams. *Science* (October 2008)

"What Do We Need to Hear a Beat? The Influence of Attention, Musical Abilities, and Accents on the Perception of Metrical Rhythm" by Fleur Bouwer (University of Amsterdam dissertation, 2016)

"Everyday Creative Activity as a Path to Flourishing" by Tamlin S. Conner, Colin G. DeYoung and Paul J. Silvia. *Journal of Positive Psychology* (November 2016)

"Well-being, Reasonableness, and the Natural Environment" by Rachel Kaplan and Stephen Kaplan. *Applied Psychology: Health and Well-Being* (Volume 3, Issue 3, 2011)

"Noticing Nature: Individual and Social Benefits of a Two-week Intervention" by Holli-Anne Passmore and Mark Holder. *Journal of Positive Psychology* (July 2016)

"A Default Mode of Brain Function" by Marcus E. Raichle, Ann Mary MacLeod, Abraham Z. Snyder, William J. Powers, Debra A. Gusnard and Gordon L Schulman. *Proceedings of the National Academy of Sciences* (January 2001)

"Awe Expands People's Perception of Time, Alters Decision Making, and Enhances Well-Being" by Melanie Rudd, Jennifer Aaker and Kathleen Vohs. *Psychological Science* (Volume 23, Issue 10, 2012)

"Vitalizing Effects of Being Outdoors and in Nature" by Richard M. Ryan, Netta Weinstein, Jessey Bernstein, Kirk Warren Brown, Louis Mistretta and Marylène Gagné. *Journal of Environmental Psychology* (Volume 30, Issue 2, 2010)

"The Role of Fingerprints in the Coding of Tactile Information Probed with a Biomimetic Sensor" by J. Scheibert, S. Leurent, A. Prevost, and G. Debregeas. *Science* (March 2009)

"Smelling Away: How the Sense of Smell can Influence our Behavior" by Lorena Vernaz Asadi. Park University (academia.edu)

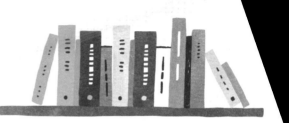

*fts of Imperfection: Let Go of
ou Think You're Supposed to Be
nbrace Who You Are* by Brené
e (Hazelden Information &
tional Services, 2010)

ow it Shapes the Brain,
the Imagination, and Invigorates
ul* by Stuart Brown
y, 2009)

*The Psychology of
nal Experience* by Mihalyi
szentmihalyi (Harper & Row,
)

*sence: Bringing Your Boldest
to Your Biggest Challenges* by
y Cuddy (Orion, 2016)

*Thanks! How the New Science of
Gratitude Can Make You Happier*
Robert A. Emmons
ghton Mifflin, 2007)

*ve 2.0: Creating Happiness and
Health in Moments of Connection* by
ara L. Fredrickson (Plume, 2013)

*rever You Go, There You Are:
ndfulness Meditation in Everyday
e* by Jon Kabat-Zinn (Hyperion,
94)

Laugh for No Reason by Madan
Kataria (Self-published, 1999)

Mindfulness by Ellen J. Langer
(Addison Wesley, 1989)

*The Organized Mind; Thinking Straight
in the Age of Information Overload* by
Daniel J. Levitin (Dutton, 2014)

*Deep Work; Rules for Focused Success
in a Distracted World* by Cal Newport
(Piatkus, 2016)

*Cooked; A Natural History of
Transformation* by Michael Pollan
(Allen Lane, 2013)

*Authentic Happiness: Using the New
Positive Psychology to Realize Your
Potential for Lasting Fulfilment* by
Martin Seligman (Nicholas Brealey,
2003)

*The Nature Fix; Why Nature
Makes Us Happier, Healthier, and
More Creative* by Florence Williams
(W.W. Norton & Company, 2017)

*Mindfulness; A Practical Guide to
Finding Peace in a Frantic World* by
Mark Williams and Danny Penman
(Piatkus, 2011)

Acknowledgments

A big thank you to all who have helped
and inspired me to make this book. Thank you
Aaldrik Jager, Maarten Vos. Thank you Irene Smit
and Astrid van der Hulst for being so supportive.
And, of course, a big thank you to Sanny van Loon,
whose illustrations make this book so
wonderful to look at.

Thank you Monica Perdoni
for asking me to make this book and being
so much fun to work with—the same goes for
Tom Kitch, Joanna Bentley, and Wayne Blades.

And thank you to my parents, Wim and Yolanda,
my lovely husband Robin, and my kids Suzy and Milo,
for always being their wonderful, creative,
now-embracing selves.